Magnolias All At Once

ISBN 978-0-935162-80-6

Singing Horse Press
5251 Quaker Hill Lane
San Diego, CA 92130

Singing Horse Press titles are available from the publisher at singinghorsepress.com or from Small Press Distribution (800) 869-7553, or at www.spdbooks.org.

At last the thought and intention of Leslie Scalapino has been captured and held gently before us on these pages, pages that are "magnolias all at once". Like Thomas Meyer's *Dao De Jing*, this is a book to keep nearby and return to often, for the acuity of its understanding. The pages, one by one, unfold into bloom. Time, the great mystery, is in the flower.

—Fanny Howe

Reading this wonderful dialogic pairing of texts, brought together in illuminating synergy of chance-assisted intention, is to find 13th century Buddhist teacher Dogen (in Norman Fischer's translation of "Uji –The Time Being") and 21st century poet Leslie Scalapino glancing at/off one another's consciousness in the coherently complementary space-time-being of their words. When Dogen says, "awakening is the koan of a living moment," I realize how often I experience just that in Scalapino's writing—in the fleeting presence of her word "events . . . floating in a sole existence, having no other manifestation," yet centrifugally evocative of the world in which we live. Surprisingly, not at all surprisingly, the same is exquisitely true of Dogen.

—Joan Retallack

Magnolias All At Once

(a text collaging quotations from
Leslie Scalapino's works with a version
of Eihei Dogen's Uji [The Time Being])

Norman Fischer

Singing Horse Press 2015

Contents

Foreword

Leslie Scalapino and I were friends for more than thirty years when she passed away after a brief illness in late May, 2010. She was a vibrant, vital, interested, interesting, and immensely important writer and person. No doubt Leslie had many closer associations with other writers and friends, but she and I shared a particular bond. Though we were quite different in temperament and the character of our work, we were equally devoted (I think this is the word) to Philip Whalen as mentor and source for our sense of writing and living. It was as if we were siblings, children of Philip — although anyone who knew Philip knows he was far from fatherly, which suited both Leslie and I quite well. Philip was (as I am) a Zen Buddhist priest, and Leslie and I, though we took it in quite different ways, also shared a devotion to Zen and Buddhism as a way of life and a source for our writing. Many of Leslie's most powerful ideas — the simultaneity of time, past present and future — the non-difference of writing and reality — the non-difference of subjectivity and objectivity—found their origins in Buddhist thought, particularly that of Nagarjuna and Dogen, whom she read again and again, with her own particular spin. These ideas dominated her critical writing and were embodied in her fiction and poetry in works whose tremendous intellectual and emotional power remains stunningly vivid in the texts she left us—as it was vivid in her powerful performances of those works in person. Leslie also practiced Zen. She practiced zazen (zen meditation) until her severe back injuries prevented it, and received Zen precepts and a Zen name from Gengo Akiba, a Japanese Master who happened to have a small temple near her home in Oakland. I gave her a second Zen name Sho Gen Rin Gyo (Illuminating Presence, Immediate Action) when I performed her funeral on July 1, 2010 at Green Gulch Farm Zen Center, where I had been abbot a decade before. Leslie's ideas on time, which were so central to her writing and to the sense she had about her life and death, came mainly from a seminal essay by the Japanese Zen Master Dogen (1200-1253) called "Uji" ("The Time Being"). This essay has also been very important to me, and I have given talks, seminars, and discussions on it often over the years. In November 2010, months after Leslie's death, I gave a seminar on the text at the Upaya Zen Center in Sante Fe, New Mexico. At that seminar I made my own faithful but somewhat free translation based on the English texts I was working from. The present volume is a version of that translation, interspersed with quotations from various of Leslie's works. The quotations were chosen by her husband, Tom White, but inserted in their places in the text by me. References works and page numbers and provenance of the original text of Dogen appear in the Acknowledgements.

I intend this short volume as an appreciation and a memorial to — and a collaboration with — my admired friend. It is wonderful that in the midst of time all time is present, making it possible for us to share again and still the writing that matters so much to us both.

Passages from Dogen are on the lef-hand page; passages from Leslie Scalapino are on the right-hand page.

"Attempts to explain the flow of time using physics rather than trying to define it away using philosophy are probably the most exciting contemporary developments in the study of time. Elucidating the mysterious flux would, more than anything else, help unravel the deepest of all scientific enigmas — the nature of the human self. Until we have a firm understanding of the flow of time, or incontrovertible evidence that it is indeed an illusion, then we will not know who we are, or what part we are playing in the great cosmic drama."

Paul Davies, *About Time: Einstein's Unfinished Revolution.*

Eihei Dogen

Leslie Scalapino

An ancient Buddha said:

> For the time being on a mountain peak
> For the time being on the ocean floor
> For the time being furious as a demon
> For the time being serene as a saint
> For the time being brilliant as a Zen Master
> For the time being dull as a stone
> For the time being a completely ordinary person
> For the time being earth, sea, and sky

cool dark cricket before moon a turquoise owl then again the owl bursts into flame flagged lit unharmed returns the cruiserweight to the dark ripples no resisting of the ripples the cruiserweight is in place rippling. (1)

For the time being means that time is being and being is time ... at least for the time being. There is no time other than being, and no being other than time, and no time other than the time being... at least for the time being. A serene saint is for the time being. Because of this time is serenely illuminated. The study of time is not abstract. Abstract study is time, but it is not about time. Time is always studied in living time. Study time in being as you are at any time, all of the time, and for the time being. Being furious as a demon is for the time being. Being sharp, being dull, being ordinary, is for the time being. Earth, sky, and sea are for the time being. Because all existence is time, nothing is separate from the twenty-four hours we are actually living every day.

In Mongolian (Tantric) Buddhist tankas (some so large as to cover an entire wall), multiple images of the same figure dispersed evenly — or different figures on multiple vertical-horizontal landscapes — are not deities, they are figures 'repeated' 'as' (to be) mind projections. As those repeat.

The repeated figures neither 'resolve' nor 'reorder' them ('itself' as repetition), but 'it' changes them.

There's no depth, it's thin, always separate. As repeated figure, there is no hierarchy.

> boat boat boat boat boat intellect boat boat
> boat boat boat boat intellect boat boat boat
> boat intellect boat boat boat boat boat boat
> intellect boat boat boat boat boat boat boat
> boat boat boat intellect boat boat boat boat
> boat boat boat boat boat intellect boat boat
> boat boat boat boat boat intellect boat boat
> boat boat boat boat boat intellect boat boat
> (2)

Although we have not rigorously examined the twenty-four hours of the day to see how long or short they are, we assume we know twenty-four hours as twenty-four hours. The traces of time having come and gone seem clear, so we do not doubt that these twenty-four hours have occurred. But though we have no doubt that time has occurred, in fact we do not know for certain, because the past is completely gone and cannot possibly be concretely verified. So, in truth, we are uncertain about each moment, as we are always uncertain about things we can't be entirely sure of. Yet it is impossible to know whether the uncertainty we experienced in the past about the past — or even the uncertainly of and about a moment ago —i s anything like the uncertainty we are experiencing now. Therefore we should be uncertain of our uncertainty — not as certain of it as we seem so often to be. Uncertainty is uncertain only for the time being. Uncertainty isn't uncertainty about something, anything, or nothing. Uncertainty is time.

If one is to move one(self) into the outside location and stay there — there is no time — and no neutrality. This is intentionality.

do anything is is antilandscape boat seamless bud is
aid bud bud bud bud bud bud bud bud bud bud bud
aid bud buds bud bud bud aid bud bud bud aid bud
do anything buds bud is antilandscape bud bud bud
aid bud bud seamless buds boat antilandscape buds
do anything buds bud is antilandscape bud bud bud
(3)

What do we mean by *me, myself?* If we contemplate this far enough, myself, my body, my position in space, and all that is involved with it, is all-inclusive — the whole world of location is involved, each and every place and thing that occupies space. And each and every place and thing — as actually being — is only for the time being.

Although it seems that things cannot occupy the same place at the same time, and so necessarily limit one another, each vying for its place in its time, in fact things do not limit each other. Time moves freely, without hindrance, and my being in this moment does not hinder your being in this moment, but embraces it. This means that love arises for the time being, the time being arises as love. In the same way, ongoing effort in spiritual practice and the joy and release of fully realized awakening to the reality of living arise as mutual functions, just as place and time function mutually... for the time being.

                    by one's figure

                                        evening

in lightning where there is no horizon, only
                              setting
moon and sun at once
axis abandoned the floating moon and sun —

              pool of horses   running
              on immense gold plain but it is indigo sky
                                        that's
              evening horses running in front of far
                                        reflecting
              water lying on the plain, pool where
                                   they're
                                   running
                                   then
              on the floor in evening and lightening
(4)

And so each of us arranges ourselves as the world. Seeing the world we see ourselves, seeing ourselves we see the world. Fully entering time, we know that we and the world mutually function as love, complete and fully embraced and resolved in our hereness... for the time being.

A characteristic of all avant-garde movements has been to change the way of seeing in a time by removing or breaking down the barrier between the spectator/reader and their being that present-time (also being in that present): To remove the barrier so that the spectator can no longer be separate from their present, from their being phenomena. This puncturing of time as space, in the conceptual space of poetry or theater, can also operate to dismantle social structuring. (5)

Understand then that variety and diversity is limitless: the world can never be encompassed objectively. Yet each and every momentary appearance encompasses the whole of the world within its appearing here. To study and experience this fact, to stop wishing for otherwise and elsewhere, or even thinking that there is or could ever be an otherwise or elsewhere, other than in those words themselves, which only mean for the time being, is the beginning of spiritual practice. *Otherwise* and *elsewhere* appear for the time being as longing.

Knowing this, stop looking for something else, for wherever you are, whatever you are, everything is included, nothing further is needed. Simply make the effort to understand what appears, recognizing that you never will understand, because appearance is too immense to be understood. The time being is awesome and illegible.

Hence there is nothing but this moment for the time being. All the time there is is all the being there is, all the myriads of worlds. Think about it — is this moment lacking in any way? In any time? In any world? Can you see that everything is here, full and complete, wherever you are? Can you feel it for the time being?

Separation of space sky rung
                          O
sun there that is outside and outside
                          itself
                          one's
walking rose only and there outside
                          rose O
at side of sky on its vertical space
                          separates

   (6)

An ordinary person with a conventional view of time under-
stands spiritual practice like this —

*At one point in time I was a deluded angry person, but later on, as a result of my
spiritual efforts, I became enlightened. That is, I went through an unfortunate
past that really existed to a really existing present in which I am now enjoying
the fruits of my spiritual endeavors. That past is far behind me now.*

But it is not that simple. In the so-called past you were you, and that
you, like all appearances, is all of time and world. The time being
appears to pass away but in fact it is always the time being. Now is
always the time being. Time is always time. It does not turn into
something else. It does not change its substance and pass into some
conceptualized realm we call the *past*. Time is always simply time —
it doesn't arrive, it doesn't exit. It's not like a scrap of discarded cloth
or a cloud in the sky that moves from peak to peak. Time is always
time. Here is always here. So your deluded past that was for the time
being is for the time being. It didn't go away. You didn't go beyond
it. You were included in it for the time being, it was included in you
for the time being. The meaning of transiency, of time as apparently
coming and going, is exactly that you are the time that is simply here
for the time being. So you should be more doubtful and more humble
about your spiritual accomplishments. You haven't changed at all.
You were simply here for the time being, you are now simply here for
the time being. And yet this is buddha, you are buddha. But this was
always buddha, you were always buddha, because buddha is always
buddha for the time being and the time being is buddha for the time
being. The time being simply swallows the time being and spits it
out. For the time being.

"The text's internal debate is the author's comparison of her mind phenomena to exterior phenomena, laying these alongside each other actually — such as the mind's comparison to dawn, to magnolias, to color of night, as if these are manifestations of mind phenomena, which they are here. Placing one's mind-actions beside magnolias (words). The same figure repeated everywhere, a line or passage may recur exactly as slipping out of, returning to, slipping out of, a frame of concentration and sound."

As text, visual image (phenomena such as black dawn and memory) and image as word are given as the same simultaneity, these (dawn, memory, optical seeing) existing separately and also abandoned as such. The implication is that if words as perception are also phenomena (if "rose" is a verb and a color at once, and if it is only a word—but is at once also a "flower") there are no images other than "dismantling itself", dismantling of (pre)conceiving seeing and thinking at once. Language could be actually shreds that are mind, rather than already socialized images (socialized images are even those phenomenally seen—which would be anything seen, such as flowers): Seeing is *there* impermanence as such.

is subjunctive — the man starving dying lying in garbage? — there not being black dawn — ?

no. not anyway — that is, anywhere, — or: subjunctive is only 'social.' both. (7)

It may be true that in the past you were deluded and angry for the time being, and that in the present you are enlightened for the time being. Yet the so-called past and the so-called present both float in the high wide and endless vista we experience as the time being. Yesterday's time and today's time do not go away. There is nowhere they could go that wouldn't also be just for the time being.

Your deluded past moves forward with you as you are. It may seem that it is far away, but it is always with you for the time being. Sometimes it may seem close, but it is even closer than it seems — it is exactly arising now. The time being is eternal unmoving time — and it is the passing hours days months and years of a lifetime. The difference is in words, in concepts, in ways we have of describing and understanding. It is not a difference in reality. Reality is only for the time being.

Riding in the car, someone else driving, the small yellow cord in one afire floats while it's night.

The yellow cord in one doesn't produce anything. The nerve is on the night, while there, so they're stilled, even. I can see the corpse.

The physical state is endless, as grasped in the light lucidity that was after the operation. That nerve is released from being afire floating in the neck.

The light coming up over the city, riding the bicycle in elation drawing the corpse behind jewel who isn't dead. On the edge of the day one realizes the eyes don't ever see. (8)

Don't think time only passes. Don't see time's passing as the only way time moves. If time only passed there would be a gap in time — you would be here and time would be there — it would have passed you by or you would have passed by it. But as you are time, and time is you, and you are here, time has not passed you and you have not passed time, you have always been you for the time being. To think of time as only passing is to misconstrue yourself — to construct a gap between yourself and yourself.

Whether they exist in the same moment, or in many different moments, all things that are are by that very fact linked to one another intimately. Whether they are the same moment or different moments, all moments are just for the time being, and it must be your time being, because you are.

In Michael McClure's work, oneself is the 'simulacra' identified as an infinite free universe. Identity is defined in his poems in terms of other entities (we are "DARK FLESH MUSIC/LAYING OUT A SHAPE," we are "INSTRUMENTS/ THAT/PLAY/ourselves," etc.). Therefore the author or the sense of self and the investigation of its desire is the pattern, which is neither present time nor the past. It is potentially infinite in form and number, as points of intuitional apprehension. (9)

The time being flows. It seems to move without accretion in an even perfect continuity.

But all these words — *continuity, flow, even, perfect,* refer to substances like water that flows by us as we stand on the banks of a stream. Such metaphors are not apt. Time isn't a flowing substance. There are no banks.

Still, what we call today flows into what we call tomorrow, today flows into yesterday, yesterday flows into today. And today flows into today, tomorrow flows into tomorrow, yesterday flows into yesterday.

Time flows smoothly, without gaps or bumps. Moments don't pile up on one another or line up end to end. Qingyuan is time, Huangbo is time, Jiangxi is time, Shitou is time, I am time, you are time, because self and other is time. Dharma relations flow in the darkness. Self and other illuminate each other as time. The ancient masters, the people of the present . . . the time being is all-inclusive, fluid, smooth. Spiritual endeavor is only for the time being. Struggling and helping is only for the time being.

In blackness millions of frogs singing on the field, hearing flying over swooping in picking them off are huge white owls — as not seeing them in the blackness one was standing at the side

experience is sole then, occurring as observing (itself) then which is also sole (in their being invisible) — the vast white owls winging planes aren't in blackness (as it is) —

aren't the observing when they are the ones seeing, as one is

to conflate blackness 'sole' 'to' starry night sky on one's interior repetition/as not being observing — or experience itself as present — that are sole.

or past — that are sole — as the voluptuous frogs imposition on blackness — only voluptuous — (as it is) observing is only occurrence (10)

Although we have views and identities and good and sensible reasons and causes for them, our views and identities are not ourselves and do not encompass the simple truth of our being here for the time being. This simple truth merely manifests itself for the time being as you and I and our views and identities. Because we don't realize this, and believe our views and identities concretely, believe we know who and what we are, who and what others and the world are, or believe in our confusion about such things, we are convinced we are ordinary persons and not enlightened buddhas.

This seems touchingly humble. But the truth is we're terrified by our awesomeness. We try to escape what we are because we think it's too much for us. But even our effort to escape manifests the time being and our immensity is never hidden. If we don't see this we need to look more deeply. The hours weeks months and years that paint a picture of a world are the constant risings and fallings, shiftings and ruminations, of the time being. Being yourself is for the time being. Being a buddha is for the time being.

Compare to the current view of 'radical questioning of subjectivity' as analysis in the writing which is (supposedly) thereby free of social construction; that is analysis (of subjectivity) which implies a critique of the conception of the unified subject. Yet as a concept of 'objectivity,' the view (the analysis) itself constitutes a unified subject.

Anyone's perception of cause and effect, and their ordering in the writing, is a conception of the unfolding of phenomena. It is oneself, and is the recreation and examination of that. There is no authority, no objectivity. (11)

The time being paints the world with light. Our anger and confusion paint the world with light. Our wisdom, our love, paint the world with light. The world paints the world with light. Light paints light with light. This is called thorough spiritual practice. Becoming a buddha through the steps and stages of a buddha's career, which include arousing compassion and commitment, practicing the virtues, becoming enlightened, entering nirvana — all this is just for the time being. It is what the time being always is, has been, will be. It's the picture of time.

My poem sequence is to reinstate (restate) experiencing in space, the mind/eye making estimations/approximations as concepts that are the same as their being in space: The language makes minute distinctions of its theme and treats these as spatial. For example, the poem-segments posit: society not based on emulations, no individual regarded as higher than another; and posit the individual perceiving in such a way — not having such feelings or behavior of emulation or sense of immanence — though (the segments posit) the individual is aware that others do, different from an animal's view. These concepts in the world, however, are not submitted to space. (In the world, concepts of feelings — such as peoples in societies feeling social values having internalized these — are not submitted to this sense of space, of no-hierarchy.) Here they are submitted to space (of no-hierarchy) to be translated to (a sense of) free space/shape/place. The format of the Granary book is accordion-like, continuous pages, that could be a horizontal scroll in that figures on a page are complete yet an extension of a limb or body on one page may appear to overlap on the next page, giving the impression that we are seeing alteration occurring in a repeated scene (or: origination in one similar). This horizontal non/narrative, as apparent overlap of images in continuous connection/action of the same or similar figures, read horizontally, is: not having hierarchy that would value one individual image above another; nor is there hierarchy of narrative as transpiring event. The language (of poem-segments) approximates a state impossible anywhere except by being in one (can't be approximated except experienced by a person). (12)

Constantly investigate the time being—there is nothing else to do. Anything else would still be the time being anyway, because we can never limit, enclose, define, know or appreciate the time being, and still it is completely the time being, because half the time being is all the time being, and even a moment missed is a moment fulfilled — as is the moment before the moment missed and the moment after because the time being is always completely fulfilled incompletely fulfilled and completely and incompletely unfulfilled. Whatever you think about it is wrong — and is nevertheless the time being itself. It is just the time being. Don't think of it as non-being. Don't think of it as the time being either.

The poem's present-time (sometimes a single word is a line, or part of a phrase is a line that as such alters the action of that phrase as it unfolds on other lines/presents-of-time), is to render the sense that 'the word' abuts sensory space that is of (in) the world. That is, 'the word,' as spatial, also makes a sense of sensory space, in relation to and different from the space of the visual world. 'The word' in its outside/space refers to and makes a sense of the undoing of social tyranny as undoing of any hierarchy in individuals' feelings and perception as well as in people's values (public indistinguishable from private). Without hierarchy, past-reality-future is apparently free paradise of childhood and of birds. 'This outside space of the word/or that is the word' abuts the other visible space of "Women being eaten by animals": (that original title of the visual images denied, however, by the fact that the female figure appears to be almost a child). The visual scene itself is denied by 'not experiencing.' The viewer (while reading beside seeing the images, but also if only seeing the visual images?) has the experience of body and mind being separated as if that is caused by the outside world. This experience of the viewer arises from their sense, in seeing, that one is separated from the scene of the girl and the animal alone together as if making love (and a sense of separation arises from the girl and animal not mimicking expressions of experiencing sensations). The disconnect/that's itself the dialogue between 'not being experienced (by the senses)' — and separation or union of mind/eye and body/sight — has to be first enacted by Smith's visual images, in order for the language to broach this (subject) matter at all. Is dialogue possible without language? (13)

We think of time as passing, but this blinds us to the fact that time never actually arrives. Even if we understood this it would only be for the time being because understanding is only for the time being. Understanding never really occurs; a moment of understanding never actually arrives.

We understand time as coming and going, we do not understand time as remaining for the time being. This is why no embodied person can understand the time being and no embodied person can experience enlightenment, which is for the time being. Even if people could recognize and embrace the time being, who could explain or express it? And even if someone could explain and express it, on and on, for a long time, that would still not be the end of the endless search for what can never be found. According to the way ordinary people understand, enlightenment and nirvana—which they take to be so important—are merely comprehensible spiritual states, passing fancies in the onrush of experiences that do not actually occur.

sometimes the brain's recycling
is broken through
in this state
of recurrence my brain
sometimes
broke through to dreams—in me

      the brain
      breaks through to
      a dream not of suffering

      in one

      dream: I

step out on top red tiered vast outside
buttes, mesas, huge red gorge with a crack
in the center pouring water-flow off
the billion stairs of the red crack forge through
which the water-flowing down billion-stairs
                  gorge   plateau
innumerable horses are running
toward me. I walked in it toward the crack
from which the horses pour
by without touching me. "They won't hurt me
/won't trample me" is a thought said
(14)

For the time being is beyond concepts and boundaries. It cannot be contained. Deva kings and heavenly beings in spirit worlds appear right and left — each of them completely exert the time being. So do you. All beings on water on land in material and nonmaterial worlds also exert the whole of the time being. So do you. All visible and invisible beings, existing and not existing, exert the whole of the time being. Each being and nonbeing does this fully — as do you. Because of your effort the time being flows on. They and you cause everything to be fully exerted, to flow. Without your effort nothing would appear, nothing would flow. Forget all your ideas about enlightenment and nirvana. How can they not be entirely incorrect, though they themselves and you as you entertain them fully exert the time being? Instead, simply study your life for the time being.

No matter 'how' one sees motions that 'appear' to be connected, the motions will be seen (by them) to reassemble the 'picture,' of 'their' reality (by which the motions are interpreted).

the sack of one's body is its changing composition (decomposition) which is without

authority, even decomposition

events are floating in a sole existence, having no other manifestation

from being produced in the series

(15)

The time being flows. But do not mistake this for movement from place to place like a rain cloud journeying east to west pressured by wind. Nor is it unmoving. The entire world is movement, there is nothing but flow.

It is like spring. In spring many things arise and flourish — the flowing beauty of constant fluctuation. In spring everything is spring — there is no place outside spring that spring could flow to or from which it has emerged. In spring there is nothing excluded from spring yet nothing can be found called spring. Spring doesn't arrive from someplace else or depart to another location when it is gone. Spring simply flows. In the same way, you flow — you should study this well.

Spring flows throughout spring. There is no corner of spring that doesn't flow as spring. But you can't find *flow* or *something that flows*. Yet spring occurs somehow — spring flows as spring, flow flows as spring, all life is springtime life. This is what we need to appreciate, this is how we need to live. Whatever you are doing, wherever you are, examine this.

When you do, you will see that there is no objective world outside or inside you—there is no vastness that encompasses you. There are no eons of time behind or before you. Your time being is neither inside nor outside. It is neither here nor elsewhere. It is not small or large. It is sufficient. To appreciate this is to appreciate the buddha way.

red leave sea in freezing (morning) — sitting in the middle of it
— that's (when inside) one freezing on red ground inner
        'walking' and 'standing' in it is the freezing (sky)
        inner as past/as being occurrence per se only
        condition of red leave sea as sky — that being
        inner as past
itself (not memory, — yet memory occurs)
        a present (events) — in freezing (dawn) is at the same
time — as — 'on red ground inner' — occurs
        so 'they're (observing and events) sole — not even occurring
        (16)

Yoashan was sent by his teacher Shitou to study with Mazu. He asked, "I am familiar with the Buddha's basic teaching. But what is the main point of Zen?"

Mazu said: "For the time being have him raise his eyebrows and wink. For the time being don't have him raise his eyebrows and wink. For the time being to have him raise his eyebrows and wink is right. For the time being to have him raise his eyebrows and wink is not right."

Hearing this, Yaoshan understood and said, "When I was studying with Shitou I was like a mosquito trying to bite an iron bull."

Mazu's expression is unique. Eyebrows and eyes are buddha activity, buddha expression, buddha transformation. *Having him raise his eyebrows and wink* is buddha activity exerted through your activity in living. Eyebrows and eyes are mountains and oceans, and mountains and oceans are eyebrows and eyes. To raise the eyebrows is to see buddha mountains in your living. To wink is to understand buddha oceans in your living. The right response flows from buddha, but is activated by your lived activity — without your lived activity there's no buddha. The wrong response doesn't mean refraining from all activity. Refraining from all activity doesn't make you or buddha wrong. Right is right and wrong is wrong — for the time being. Right and wrong, activity and non activity — all for the time being.

I asked Whalen if his writing was the same as meditation: that is, if his writing was doing the same thing as the process of meditation as the 'disjunctive present' which is no-separation of self and outside, and does not form these (self or outside) either. He answered no, that writing is writing and meditation is itself. I take that to mean: Language is always an ordering device. Language can't be the same as a state that does not rely upon any device and creates no entity, can't be a state that hasn't even language to rely upon (which is the characteristic of meditation). If the subject of writing is 'being only a disjunctive present,' the writing is not doing that, it would merely reproduce subject matter and division from it. Yet I think Whalen was using language to make being outside even what language is, let alone its conventional usage, while his poetry is based in language's daily usage as speaking, thinking and fantasizing. The Beats as a movement were undertaking to undo convention of U.S. 'seeing' which continually reproduces 'being' divided from subject matter as subject matter. Whalen undertook that 'undoing' as the process of the language itself. (17)

Mountains are for the time being, oceans are for the time being. If not, there would be no mountains and oceans. Don't think of mountains and oceans as things, and time as an element in which they abide. There are no things and there is no time but the time being that is arising now in the visible and invisible world that flows with your lived activity. If there were another time outside of time such a time would swallow the time being and mountains and oceans would be swallowed. Time would be cancelled. Mountains and oceans would dissolve. But time cannot be cancelled. Mountains and oceans arise.

This is why Buddha awakens to the morning star and holds a spring-time flower aloft. Seeing this flower, Mahakasyapa raises his eyebrows. Buddha winks. This is all simply for the time being every moment of the time being. This is the depth, the suchness, the isness, the echo, of time, all of time, all of the time — for the time being.

The Dihedrons Gazelle-Dihedrals Zoom was written by words being chosen at random from the dictionary in a process of alexia, not as mental disorder but word-blindness — to make an unknown future — yet making as it happens sensual exquisite corpses led to the discovery that there isn't any future, isn't even any present. Such an exquisite corpse, read, is in an instant yet not even in 'a present.' Outside's events unite gluing to each other a single object. That which had already existed is by chance. The exquisite corpses are physical as if one such is flesh-butterfly-other- (real-time events such as the attack on Mumbai), each such event-cluster internally hybrid rather than being separate presentation as idea. That is, the writing is not the idea of the whole framework of occurrences after without its existence ever being. In the accumulating stream of events, hybrids repeating parts of an event in different combinations, the parts rearranged by imagination begin to pierce each other surpassing single outlines and boundaries, the sense of infinite combinations are actions bliss. *That which had already existed* is by chance: not only includes events in real-time but visual scenes existing before the writing — Jess's collages that show parts of the reality though different scenes of it infinitely un- folding as randomly discovered composite actions. Masami Teraoka's painting of an octopus sucking a woman's front was a memory occurring simultaneous with the instant of writing it: is seeing our memories making the present. The characters have this sensual memory though they are without memory unknown sensual object as it comes up found by its language, its being at once

(18)

One day Zen Master Guixiang said, "For the time being awakening arrives, but not expression. For the time being expression arrives but not awakening. For the time being both awakening and expression arrive. For the time being neither awakening nor expression arrive."

Both awakening and expression are for the time being. Both the arrival of awakening and expression and the non-arrival of awakening and expression are for the time being. Before a moment arrives, its non-arrival has arrived. Any moment is here when it is here, here before it is here, here after it is here. Awakening is a donkey, clumsy and confused. Expression is a horse, elegant and bright. The grunt work of spiritual practice in the trenches is awakening. The galloping frolic of the Zen Masters' words and actions is expression. Being full of the teaching is expression. Never having been empty of the teaching is awakening. Awakening is expression. Grunting or galloping, then and now, yesterday and today, accomplishment and non-accomplishment, are all just pictures of the time being.

Arriving doesn't mean you've come from elsewhere. Not having arrived doesn't mean you're not already there.

R-hu ends on a note of wonder — What would a text be like if it could drop all framing devices, have none — for there aren't any such frames in phenomenal reality? — not even sound-structures or resonance, nothing on which to pin narrative or place, and no place by which it could orient itself or form directions — not a vacuum either, being utter freedom? (19)

The time being is like this. A moment is completely overwhelmed by its arrival but not by its non-arrival. Before and after are completely overwhelmed by before and after — but not by an arriving moment now. Awakening overwhelms awakening and awakens itself. Expression overwhelms expression and expresses itself. Overwhelming overwhelms overwhelming and overwhelms itself. This is why we understand neither time nor ourselves: every moment is completely overwhelmed by itself. Awakened, we don't know it. Expressing, we have no idea. And it goes on this way — overwhelming overwhelms overwhelming and overwhelms overwhelming overwhelming overwhelming. Everything is overwhelmed — completely what it is with absolutely nothing left over. There's no place to stand and look. No applause, no congratulations. For the time being.

Text-thangkas that are no-image (voiding by repetition of the same image) are my text-imitation of Buddhist wall-hangings that multiply repeat the same figure; theirs with a Buddhist connotation, yet as present-time daily conceiving-also visually-they're akin (in my essay) to Andy Warhol's multiple portraits of the same person, such as his repetitions of single head (such as Elizabeth Taylor). Obviously this is not the same as the repetition of the figure of Buddha, yet I'm emphasizing 'empty' figure being states of action practice of seeing as voiding. The thangkas may repeat a figure in scenes of the landscape in which the people live. The surface and repetition of my text-thangkas are intended to be transparency devoid of critique and are neither self-conscious perception, nor lineage. (20)

And all of this is you, is activated by your living, so no existence is not also you, and you are all of existence. This is why you are always meeting someone. This is why someone is always meeting someone. This is why you are always meeting you. This is why meeting is always meeting meeting. This is deep time, time's reverberating echo, the endlessness of time for the time being.

Around that time, the magnolia trees began to bloom, and taking a nap one day I struggled out of sleep to drive up the highway ramp with the magnolia blossoms roiling without movement ahead. They were in the center of that sleep, which was in the past but still there. Left over itself, and my out ahead in the car with the roiling magnolia blossoms everywhere on the earth. (21)

Awakening is the koan of living a moment, the awesome wonder of being alive. Expressing this wonder is simply going forward in living—opening the door that is always before you. Every moment arriving brings complete freedom and letting go. Every moment not yet arriving carries everything in its fullness, which is its absence. Whatever comes, whatever doesn't come, is just for the time being.

comparing the mind to magnolias
or to sky, because one sees.
but comparing people's actions to sky
or to war to moon outside? is in that space
then.
apprehend
behavior-evening - ferocity even
from just one - where there was no reason
bewildering - doesn't seem
'bewildering' if it's huge in multitude.
indentation so that they're even
one to evening – is no behavior-evening
any event a random space
(22)

This is what the old masters said. Is there anything to add? Awakening and expression — even part way — is for the time being. Awakening and expression not even as far as part way — also for the time being. Part of the time being and not even part of the time being is all of the time being, all of the time.

So — no matter how much or how little you can make of yourself or your life—practice for the time being.

To have him raise his eyebrows and wink is only half the time being.

To have him raise his eyebrows and wink completely misses the time being.

Not to have him raise his eyebrows and wink is only half the time being.

Not to have him raise his eyebrows and wink completely misses the time being.

There's no use looking for standards or assessing levels of comprehension or realization. There's no achievement or comparison. There's never arrival or non-arrival; there's always arrival and non-arrival. So enjoy the conceptual knots endemic to having a human mind, but do not pull them tighter. Instead, practice thoroughly, live fully, and see. Let things come and let them go. Let a moment arrive and let a moment not arrive. To be open in all of this is to live the time being—but you have always lived the time being.

The figure, loose, black hair, ahead on a motorcycle is silent.
It is soft black circle, clap flattening the sky.

Already, actions occur before. Which are solidified and which
aren't that when occurring at the same time. I.e. when occurring.

Oneself as a child with others ahead of one on the road. All
swaying dash furiously on bicycles in rain rolls of thunder flattening
the black sky. The people are not in visible light. Lightning hits the
road over and over in front of the zigzagging bicycles which are then
visible.

The lightning hits right in front of them in the rain coming
down. The sheets of rain are somewhat warm. Yet alongside it is the
black Arctic Ocean.

Thin bicycles in the heavy rain, the weighing sheet of the
black Arctic Ocean is alongside. Since this is 'when one is a child
dashing on a bicycle in lightning' it is dislocated, and because it is
such or is anything will not be known. (23)

Coda

Where are you at any moment and where am I? The thin story of your being who and where you are is completely torn. Those withdrawn into their absences call out, which is their being here with you. Your touching them in time answers their calls, is your calling to them that is answered by them in their and your being for the time being.

>   not the day being within the blossom
>   as in reverse (rather than the day in it)—the blossom
>   isn't in the day either
>   'not a black dawn/a black dawn' is real-time only.
>   (24)

Afterword

The essay Uji ("The Time Being") can be found in the first volume of Kazuaki Tanahashi's two volume translation of Dogen's text *Shobogenzo* (under the English title *Treasury of the True Dharma Eye*, Shambhala Publications, 2010). There are several other English versions available. As far as I know, no other Buddhist teacher has written directly about time per se. Writing in the thirteenth century, Dogen's categories of expression are of course traditional, but his radical flexibility in the use of them, and the expansiveness of his chief themes, make his work seem strikingly contemporary.

Dogen Kigen (1200-1253) was the founder of Japanese Soto Zen and is universally ranked among the greatest of Buddhist thinkers and writers, transcending his tradition. In Japan, certainly, he is unparalleled as a religious thinker, philosopher and literary genius. His unique writing style is notoriously playful, difficult, and profound, and he is the first Japanese to write philosophical texts in the colloquial language, rather than the traditional Chinese. His importance in Buddhist thought and literature is probably most analogous to Augustine in the West, though Dogen lived roughly a thousand years later. *Shobogenzo*, his master work, has been legendary for centuries. At first unpublished, and known only to adepts and disciples, the text was later brought to light and venerated, but for centuries almost never read. During the Tokugawa period (1603-1868), the text was unearthed, edited, and published in its entirety and used as the basis for a radical reformation of Soto Zen during the period when Japan was self-consciously entering into dialog with the West. In the twentieth century, secular Japanese philosophers touted *Shobogenzo* as their answer to the great Western philosophies (Japan, until that point, not having what is called "philosophy"). Today, *Shobogenzo* stands almost alone among Buddhist writings as a work that philosophers and intellectuals with or without Buddhist affiliations take seriously. Its startlingly contemporary style (Dogen often sounds post-modern in his playful linguistic paradoxes and summersaults) and themes (in addition to time, Dogen writes extensively of language, being, space, etc.) have invited comparison in scholarly essays and books to Heidegger, Wittgenstein, and others. Naturally, contemporary Soto Zen practitioners, both here and in Japan, have embraced *Shobogenzo* as the basis for their practice.

Fascinated with Dogen's writing, I began studying him when there was at yet very little available in English. His work was the subject of my graduate thesis in 1975, and I have been reading and pondering it since then.

Acknowledgments

My free version of Dogen's text Uji ("For the Time Being," 1240) is based mainly on the English version translated by Kakuazi Tanahashi. It appears in his two volume translation of Dogen's great work *Shobogenzo* (*Treasury of the True Dharma Eye*, Shambhala, 2010) as Fascicle 12 Volume One, p 104.

Quotations from Leslie Scalapino's Works:

(1) From: *The Dihedrons Gazelle-Dihedrals Zoom* (The Post-Apollo Press, 2010), page 104.
(2) From: *HOW PHENOMENA APPEAR TO UNFOLD* Chapter: SEAMLESS ANTILANDSCAPE (Litmus Press, 2011), page 273.
(3) From: *Seamless Antilandscape* (Spectacular Books, (1999), page 20.
(4) From: *It's go in / quiet illumined grass / land* (The Post-Apollo Press, 2002), page 40.
(5) From: *HOW PHENOMENA APPEAR TO UNFOLD* Chapter: LANGUAGE AS TRANSIENT ACT, page 129.
(6) *From It's go in / quiet illumined grass / land* Page 7.
(7) From: *Day Ocean State of Stars Night* (Green Integer, 2007), page 121.
(8) From: *HOW PHENOMENA APPEAR TO UNFOLD* Chapter: THE FRONT MATTER, DEAD SOULS, page 241.
(9) From: *HOW PHENOMENA APPEAR TO UNFOLD* Chapter: PATTERN—AND THE 'SIMULACRAL', page 22.
(10) From: *Green and Black, Selected Writings* (Talisman, 1996), pages 92-93.(11)

(11) From: *HOW PHENOMENA APPEAR TO UNFOLD*, page 121.

(12) From: *HOW PHENOMENA APPEAR TO UNFOLD* Chapter: THE DIVISION BETWEEN FACT AND EXPERIENCE, pages 183-184.

(13) From: *HOW PHENOMENA APPEAR TO UNFOLD* Chapter: THE DIVISION BETWEEN FACT AND EXPERIENCE, pages 183-184.

(14) From: *Flow-Winged Crocodile* (Chax Press, 2010), pages 32-33.

(15) From: *Green and Black, Selected Writings*, page 9.

(16) From: *Green and Black, Selected Writings*, pages 92-93.

(17) From: *HOW PHENOMENA APPEAR TO UNFOLD* Chapter: LANGUAGE AS TRANSIENT ACT, page 133.

(18) From: *The Dihedrons Gazelle-Dihedrals Zoom;* Author's Note, pages vii-viii.

(19) From: *HOW PHENOMENA APPEAR TO UNFOLD* Chapter: THE INTERIOR EXPERIENCE OF BEING/ SOCIALLY CONSTRUCTED, page 259.

(20) From: *HOW PHENOMENA APPEAR TO UNFOLD* Chapter: THE INTERIOR EXPERIENCE OF BEING/ SOCIALLY CONSTRUCTED, page 259.

(21) From: *HOW PHENOMENA APPEAR TO UNFOLD* Chapter: TRANSCRIPTION – (OR LINEAGE) AS VISUAL, page 288.

(22) From: *It's go in / quiet illumined grass / land*, page 7.

(23) From: *R-hu* (Atelos Press, 2000), page 13.

(24) From: *HOW PHENOMENA APPEAR TO UNFOLD* Chapter: IMAGE/WORD IN CROWD AND NOT EVENING OR LIGHT AND THE TANGO, page 154.

Interview

[The following interview between Norman Fischer and Paul Naylor was conducted via email with the intent to give readers who are unfamiliar with either Eihei Dogen or Leslie Scalapino an angle or two of approach to *Magnolias All At Once.*]

PN: Hi Norman. I thought we'd begin with the occasion for *Magnolias All At Once,* your friendship with Leslie Scalapino. How and when did that friendship begin?

NF: Impossible to say exactly, partly because we knew each other for such a long time and partly because I don't have a great memory. In the 1970's the Bay Area poetry community was very lively — as it is now — but there were not as many people as there are now. So people knew one another, saw each other at readings and events, there was a sense of knowing people even when you didn't know them so well. A common purpose and sensibility. So that people like Leslie and I, involved with the same kind of writing, would surely know one another. It would be automatic. And then too we were both friends of and devotees of Philip Whalen, and we had a mutual interest in Buddhist thought. When I first knew her, Leslie was living with Rick Duerdon, who was part of the Beat Writer's generation, and a friend of Philip's, and her first publisher was Jack Shoemaker, who also published Snyder and Robert Aitken, who was a Zen teacher of mine — many family associations. So in my mind it's impossible to separate my knowing Leslie from my own development as a writer, from all the thoughts, ideas, experiences, and relationships I was engaged in at the time. Leslie was unique, a very serious and unusual writer, and this was immediately apparent. I was always amazed by Leslie's work, always interested in it. But, yes, I would like to know when and how I first met Leslie! I would like to have an organized story about our relationship! But I don't. (This is maybe very much in keeping with the theme of *Magnolias All At Once*).

PN: In your Foreword, you write that many of Leslie's most powerful ideas derive from Buddhist thought; I'm particularly interested in how you see the idea of "the simultaneity of time" working in her writing and how that idea resonates with Dogen's "Uji." Perhaps it would be helpful if you first give us a sense of what the "simultaneity of time" means in Buddhism in general and in Dogen in particular.

NF: Big question! There are many Buddhist teachings not about time per se that have implications for notions of time. Early concepts of Buddhist momentariness (that there is nothing that actually exists as such: everything is just a momentary flashing in and out of existence) eventually led to the emptiness teachings, which say that everything, in its momentariness, is empty, non-existent, without substance or reality in the sense we project. If this is so, then what is time? Essentially there is no time. Time and being become the same phenomenon (this is what "Uji" means — being/time or time/being, or, as is often translated, colloquially, as Dogen meant it, For the Time Being). Later developments in Buddhist thought, especially in China, developed the idea of all-inclusiveness and simultaneity. That is, no moment of time is a discreet separate moment; every moment includes all of time. As time, so space. Every point in space includes all of space all of the time.

The famous *Avatamsaka Sutra*, which is the basis for this philosophy, has dizzying passages about the simultaneous appearance of myriad Buddhas on every particle of space constantly (eternally) teaching the dharma. This is the idea behind the intensity of Zen practice — you sit down in meditation at the center of the universe in the middle of the single eternal inexistent moment of time that always and never exists. Dogen grew up on all this, and was the only Buddhist thinker I am aware of who wrote explicitly about time and what all this meant for our notions of time. (He also has an essay called "Space").

Leslie certainly was aware of all this. But she started with her own intuitive sense of it, and reading Buddhism only helped to crystallize her thinking, that was already developed. My guess is that it was Leslie's experience, from her childhood, that the outside and the inside were the same thing. That what she was feeling/experiencing inside was the same as what was going on outside. And that it was all happening in one simultaneous moment, which she identified as the moment of writing. Her last two novels enact this fully. For Leslie the world was taking place inside her thought/writing and her thought/writing was the world itself — and all of it was happening all of the time. So that every moment was completely decisive. This is her utter uniqueness — a writer almost impossibly, hermetically, inward and at the same time as social and political as it is possible to be — and seeing the two not as contradictory but as the same thing, not only for her, but as reality.

PN: And a big answer! If every moment does include all of time — past, present, and future — simultaneously, then any attempt to present that simultaneity in acts of writing will be inherently paradoxical, since writing necessarily, to at least a minimal extent, has to appear successively—one word follows another, one line follows another, one sentence follows another, etc. Much of modernist writing has, of course, focused on ways of working around that linear dimension of language. What strategies do you see Dogen and Scalapino using to circumvent the linear conventions of writing? Unlike Leslie, Dogen, who lived in the 13th century C.E., didn't have the precedents of modernism to work with, so I'm particularly interested in ways you see him negotiating those linear conventions of writing.

NF: Well this is another terrific question. It makes me think it would be interesting to spend the next few years looking in detail at texts by Leslie and Dogen and actually trying to sort out how they do it. A worthwhile study I am sure, but one that I probably am not going to get to anytime soon. So let me instead be broad and general in my response.

I guess I would be hard pressed to create an exhaustive list of the various modernist inventions to circumvent the linear nature of language. But whatever they are (stream of consciousness, dream or automatic writing, fractured narrative, exquisite corpse, use of multiple voices, paratactical structures, cut ups, etc) there are certainly many more Leslie used and invented. In fact, I think Leslie didn't use any of the usual stuff. In a sense, I would say, she was too pure, too naive, in a way, to knowing make use of things invented by others. My impression of her method is that she worked from the inside out; that is, she didn't think about how language works and figure out or adapt strategies to stretch it; instead she had an inner compulsion to express something that occurred to her (that usually, I believe, came from her experiences of suffering in the so-called external world) that could only be expressed in new forms of writing. So without necessarily figuring out what these new forms were, she simply began expressing what she felt she needed to, which automatically came out in new forms. So, for instance, syntax as we know it went out the window. Leslie's writing is notably written in a hybrid or anyway weird syntax in which connections are always unclear or unconventional. Syntax makes the hierarchy of the parts of language clear, which makes meaning clear. But Leslie is against any form of hierarchy, so against normative syntax. She often uses repeated phrases that seem haunting or haunted and also impossible to tell exactly what they mean. Although a good reader of her work knows what they mean without being able to explain. Then there is her use of repetition, very much influenced by her reading of Stein, but also completely unlike Stein. Like Leslie, Stein is possessed by her writing, but Stein is playful and funny and cute in ways that Leslie never is. Leslie is always urgent. Not that she doesn't have a sense of humor, she does, but somehow her humor is so off the charts of the conventional mind-set that you can never be sure when how or if she is being funny. Then there's her use of neologism, very odd lineation in poetry, genre-bending strategies, and so on.

In the case of Dogen's writing you have a host of completely different factors involved. For one thing, Dogen is writing either in Chinese or medieval Japanese, languages I don't know, though I did study Chinese a little as a graduate student. Chinese has no grammar to speak of, no verb conjugations, no parts of speech — just ideograms whose relational meaning is determined largely by context. So there's a lot of ambiguity and word play automatically present, if you want to notice it. Japanese is built on Chinese ideograms with Japanese phonetic letters added to indicate parts of speech and inflection, so that there is explicit sentence structure. Dogen's great work *Shobogenzo* (Treasure of the True Dharma Eye, which includes his essay on time) is one of the first literary works written in Japanese (before that, Japanese people wrote in Chinese, much as Europeans wrote in Latin) — which gave Dogen enormous leeway to figure out how to mine this Chinese-Japanese axis. He was constantly playing around, stretching everything, mistranslating from Chinese, using the discrepancies between the languages to his advantage to obscure and expand meaning. On top of this is the fact that Zen language — which in Dogen's time was a specialty patois in Chinese, but not yet in Japanese, because Dogen was one of the first Zen people in Japan — had already developed numerous literary strategies to fracture a reader's sense of explanatory or conventional meaning.

In his extensive introduction to his two-volume translation of *Shobogenzo*, Kaz Tanahashi lists no less than 13 methodologies for deranging ordinary language that Zen invented and Dogen elaborated on, among them, (7) "contrasted meaning" (using the same words or phrases to mean different things), (3) "Tautology" ("a fish swims like a fish, a bird flies like a bird");and (8) "opposite use of the same metaphor." To this range of strategies Dogen adds mistranslation, misreading, claiming to understand something as the opposite of what it is usually understood to mean, random combining of words and phrases in semi-systematic style, and elaborately rhetorical insistence on seemingly absurd conceptions. In all this, Dogen's intention is not to be cute or outrageous: in fact Dogen wasn't a Zen trickster type at all, he was a conservative cleric who ran monasteries and communities and considered himself to be completely orthodox. His point was that ordinary syntax and grammar and ordinary thinking and conceptualization — even of Buddhist doctrinal teaching — was essentially imprisoning, misleading, and incorrect. He wanted to communicate joy, liberation, and flexibility with language, and in order to do that he had to erode language, constantly creating doubt — while, at the same

70

time, being virtually the only Zen Master in history who was actually, primarily, a writer, and who validated language as essential religious experience.

PN: One of the major strategies modernists used to circumvent the linear conventions of writing and the concept of time that underlies those conventions was collage. You describe *Magnolias All At Once* as "a text collaging quotations from Leslie Scalapino's works and a version of Eihei Dogen's "Uji" [The Time Being]." Did you choose collage as a form in order to foreground the understanding of the simultaneity of time that Dogen and Leslie share? And was your choice of collage as a form for this text influenced by the almost eight hundred year gap between the times in which your two subjects wrote?

NF: I am afraid I am not as sophisticated as all that. Influenced, certainly, by my contemporaries and forebears in recent genera-tions, I have used all sorts of techniques in my writing to find in-teresting meaning. Collage, cut up, appropriation, various other operations. Just like anyone these days. These techniques are now commonplace, items in the toolbox. So you automatically use them. I know that some writers think about what techniques to use and how those techniques reflect the work they are trying to do and maybe the social, political, or psychological issues they are dealing with in the work. I don't really think about any of that. I just usu-ally (as in the case of *Magnolias*) stumble into something by chance and then I have a feeling about it and continue to stumble forward trusting I'll end up someplace I want or need to go. Most of my poems start with something I stumble into. I have written long poems I never intended to write just because I stumbled into something and then stumbled forward a little more, and at some point became committed to following the form that emerged. I assume I am not unique in this. In this particular case I actually wasn't writing a literary work, I was doing a weekend workshop on Dogen's text and in the course of doing that I made the translation just for the fun of it. It seemed a worthwhile piece, so I fiddled around with it, refining it. But had no idea of doing anything with it: there are plenty of scholarly translations of "Uji" and I am not a scholar. Then I had the thought that Leslie loved this text and that her work everywhere reflects it, so wouldn't it be lovely to put the two together. But how go through her enormous output and find the right passages? That was a bit daunting. So I asked Tom White, Leslie's husband of many years, who was always (though he is a scientist, with no literary training I am aware of) very interested in her work, and had a very good eye for it, to choose the quotations. Tom is now a Zen practitioner with our local Bay Area Zen group and is quite interested in Dogen's text himself, and has his own scientific take on it, which is quite interesting. So he was the perfect person for this job. He selected a sheaf of Leslie quotations and I, again simply by feel, without too much thought, stuck them into the Dogen text where it felt to me they ought to go. While all this may sound lazy and haphazard (which it is!) I also have a theory about it. If Cage and Mac Low and others can use "chance operations" to create works, why can't I or anyone else just use chance per se, without any operations. Found words, found poems, found circumstances. Passing random thoughts etc. Their theory was that ego was too confining and that chance operations would circumvent ego to expand the sphere of the work. But I have been practicing zazen throughout my career as a poet. You might say, in fact, that practicing zazen is foundational to my poetics. That the silence of zazen echoes throughout my works. This of course doesn't mean I don't have an ego, or am not limited by an ego, but probably it does mean I am not quite as mesmerized by my ego as possibly Cage and Jackson were at the time they devised their chance operation procedures and committed themselves to them. My ego probably has a lot of holes in it and parts where it is worn through or slightly tattered, so chance can bleed in and impulse might not be quite as ego-determined, may be more intuitive, in a broad sense (that is, attuned to reality rather than just to myself). This may or may not be true, but at least it is a good theory to justify what comes naturally and easily to me!

PN: In your Foreword, you write that Leslie repeatedly read Nagarjuna and Dogen "with her own particular spin." I imagine we'll discuss her "spin" on Dogen as we move through the text of *Magnolias*, but I was wondering what her "spin" on Nagarjuna was?

NF: As always with Leslie, it's hard to tell whether she got to where she was by following Nagarjuna, or whether she was already there and found a partner, and an explanation, in Nagarjuna. I guess the latter. This is not to say that I find her reading of Nagarjuna skewed, quirky, or incorrect. In fact, as far as I can tell, she got Nagarjuna exactly right. Yet when you read her explication of Nagarjuna, it comes out Leslie. And it turns out that Nagarjuna's thought is the perfect foundation — the obvious foundation — for Leslie's work. Understanding her reading of Nagarjuna helps a lot in appreciating what Leslie is doing.

Her most direct explication is found in her essay "The Recovery of the Public World," that's in her book *The Public World/Syntactically Impermanent* (Wesleyan University Press, 1999). In fact, that book features an epigraph written by Leslie that refers to Nagarjuna : "As: Nagarjuna's 'destruction of all philosophical views' — obviously this would include all modes of articulation, and any definitions of procedures of 'discourse.'" In other words, as the book argues in many ways, all rules, all standards, all hierarchies, all prescriptions are incorrect and must be strenuously rejected.

In the essay, Leslie begins with a brief explication of Nagarjuna's thought (citing three key books by/about him in a footnote), then illustrates what she takes from Nagarjuna by discussing the work of Robert Grenier, Robin Blaser, and Mei-mei Berssenbrugge — writers who had been important to her throughout her career. For Leslie, Nagarjuna's thought makes clear (and seems completely irrefutable, because it does so little, and says nothing!) that there is nothing stable, that holds up, that's not empty, and therefore constantly to be questioned, constantly to be moving. So that language, and therefore writing, can never stand still. I suppose this is Leslie's most basic take — that there isn't anything per se, that writing is the making of reality for the human mind, it's the investigation or instigation of reality. Writing isn't just edifying, a commentary, a cultural product. It's much more crucial than that. So Leslie resisted all kinds of ideologies and ideas of avant-garde writing as political, in the narrow sense, or cultural. And she rejected just as strenuously ideas of "experience" or "personhood," as if these were sensible things. She was always opposing writers and ideas that would have appeared to be allies — because she was resisting anything that was being set up as something, even if she was in favor of that something. And she resisted mightily the idea that "difficult" texts, such as those she wrote, were elitist, or irrelevant. For her the writing she did and was interested in was at the heart of human reality. Not marginal! "Nagarjuna's 'mode' as a model of 'poetic writing' implies demonstration, which is both (and mutually exclusive— at once) demonstration of thought and demonstration of action. This implies an enjambment of states or conditions of reality. Writing that is either a 'lyrical expressivity' or convention

74

of discourse cannot be receptive to these conditions." (p 56). Later in the essay (p 61), she writes: "The content of phenomena is scrutiny, according to Berssenbrugge." Though attributed here to Berssenbrugge, that idea is Leslie's central and most passionate thought. Everything is empty, without any actual fixed existence. Therefore to look, to engage, to scrutinize, is the actual content of reality. There is no content other than the effort to scrutinize.

PN: Nagarjuna is well-known for distinguishing between two levels or dimensions of truth: conventional and ultimate. Although he argues stridently that these two levels are interrelated and inseparable — that they do not constitute an ontological or epistemological dualism — it does seem that the role of language on the path of enlightenment is restricted to the conventional level or dimension. It seems that, in relation to the ultimate level of truth, language, for Nagarjuna, can only inform us of its incapacity to address that level. Although I suspect Leslie and Dogen would agree with Nagarjuna's position, they seem to have a more capacious sense of what language can do. Both embrace the poetic dimension of language in ways that Nagarjuna doesn't. I'm particularly interested in how they might use language to express, to use Leslie's phrase, "an enjambment of states or conditions of reality." Do you see Leslie and Dogen doing that? If so, how does each go about it?

NF: Yes certainly Leslie and Dogen are doing that. And this book itself is a case in point! In it we have Dogen's words, Leslie's words, expressing the inexpressible. As you say, following Nagarjuna, one might conclude that there's very little point in speaking or writing, because such acts of language are always limited to relative (read "less important") reality. And one can read much of Zen literature (but not Dogen) to be saying that: "Truth is beyond language." But this misses what Nagarjuna (as you correctly point out) is actually saying: that relative and absolute truth do not constitute a duality. They are just different language or perspective. Just as the Heart Sutra says: form (relative) is emptiness (absolute); but emptiness is form. And much of Zen thought deals with this teaching, emphasizing and expanding it. This means that all expressions of relative reality are also expressions of absolute reality. And that language can and always does express what language can't express! When you know this (as Dogen and Leslie do) you produce texts like the one we have here. Texts that, on the one hand, can seem opaque or at least very odd, but that are in fact quite clear and eloquent in their expression of what's beyond or underneath — which is to say deeply inside — language and human experience.

You ask how Leslie and Dogen go about creating their forms of expression. Dogen of course is a faithful traditional Buddhist from Medieval Japan. So he writes in the framework of Buddhist discourse. The basic thrust of his writing is deconstruction. He is always taking normative Zen and Buddhist teachings and subjecting them to language operations that have the effect of taking the teachings apart — pointing out, demonstrating, really, rather than explaining, that these teachings are inherently self-contradictory and, when scrutinized carefully, collapse of their own weight. But he's also saying that such collapse, far from obviating the teachings' virtue, brings forth its actual essence! Dogen is a essentially a philosopher, but his style of expression is more poetic or intuitive than discursive, since, as I've said above, the Chinese and Japanese philosophical traditions are written and thought in uninflected languages that don't produce the kind of writing we ordinarily think of as philosophical.

Leslie, on the other hand, is a poet, so she's concerned with form, genre, the feeling and flavor of words and their structures per se. Her language is much more various and adventuresome. She's also a philosopher so there is plenty of Dogen-like expression in her work. Both Dogen and Leslie have a powerful and passionate feeling about the world, about reality, that moves them. That feels urgent. What makes their work so strong is that you feel that urgency throughout. Their works are struggles, really, to express that urgency — whose nature is precisely that it presses on the boundaries of the expressible, reaching for the inexpressible.

PN: "Language can and always does express what language can't express": I love that sentence! And you're right, this book, *Magnolias All At Once*, is an instance of that happening on the page. With that in mind, I'd like to turn our attention to the book itself. As you said in your Foreword, Tom White chose the passages from Leslie's work, and you paired those passages with your translations of Dogen's essay "Uji," so I'd like you to walk us through a few of those pairings. I'm particularly interested in how you "read" the dialog between Dogen and Leslie in those particular pairings. Let's start with the pairing on pages 22 and 23. What compelled you to place these two pages together?

NF: I like this particular pairing particularly. Dogen is talking about how we actually exist in the world — how we could be experiencing our lives if we opened up to the way they really are (that is, as Dogen sees it) rather than the way our stupid and cramped conceptual frameworks (which are of course in great part socially determined) condition us to see it. So Dogen here is making a broad metaphysical pronouncement. When he ends his statement (at least in my version!) with repeating the phrase "for the time being" he's saying "and don't make my metaphysical pronouncement into a big reification, imprisoning you all over again. Anything true is only true for the time being."

Leslie's short text is about avant-garde writing and how its methods and goals actually promote the experience of appreciation, in the reader, of the metaphysical situation that Dogen is pointing to. "To remove the barrier so that the spectator can no longer be separate from their present, from their being phenomena." That is, experiencing the literary work can actually do this, can break down barriers of cramped thinking and feeling, so that we can be more who we actually are. "This puncturing of time as space, in the conceptual space of poetry or theater, can also operate to dismantle social structuring." This sentence reminds me of Adorno, whom I've been reading lately, who says that social structures are in part created by and can be changed by consciousness. So experiencing avant-garde works can not only change us, change our consciousness, but change the social structures inside and outside us. This little passage beautifully encapsulates Leslie's passionate and ambitious mission for her work and, as it relates to Dogen, might be the clearest example in *Magnolias All at Once* of how writing, for Leslie, can demonstrate and be a path toward the realization of Dogen's teaching.

PN: The idea that an investigation of time/being can inaugurate changes in both consciousness and social structures is striking. The pairing on pages 38 and 39 digs deeper into that investigation, so I'd like you to comment on that pairing. What would you say "moves between" Dogen and Leslie here?

NF: This is very difficult, mostly because exactly what these passages are telling us is that commenting on how this works is always a mistake; that is, whatever you say is going to be both wrong, in that your comment will never be true, and right, in that your comment, false though it will surely be, will in any case be a demonstration (if not an explanation) of the point. Dogen: "Whatever you think about it is wrong." But what would happen if we really understood that whatever we think about anything is wrong, yet everything is, anyway, right? And that we have to, somehow, include this fact in our thinking? Consciousness would change drastically — people would find it much more difficult to be self-righteous and cruel, to grasp for control over others. It would be impossible not to have a light touch and a sense of humor about everything! Leslie then (in this juxtaposition, and maybe in life too) takes this basic fact and applies it specifically to the task of making poetic texts. As if poetic texts could have a useful function in bringing about this sort of change, could be educational. (Anyway, regardless of that, as a poet, one has to make texts and so naturally wants to make them in accord with the deepest sense of reality, and maximum altruism, that one can muster.)

Leslie's comments here are complicated. They refer to a specific work of hers, a collaborative book, her words with Kiki Smith's drawings, *The Animal Is In The World Like Water In Water*. (Granary Books, 2010). So when she talks about the word "abutting sensory space," she's referring literally to the pages of the book, in which her words actually do abut the visual space of Kiki's drawings, but also extending this to the world outside the drawings (the drawings are representational, of the outer world, of an animal variously eating or biting, in a rather matter of fact way, a naked woman). The piece's title refers to George Bataille's *The Theory of Religion*, a great text that I also once used for an essay Leslie published some years before 2010, in her magazine Enough. Maybe that's how she got onto it, I don't know. So there's a lot of background and detail behind her comments here. Maybe a gesture toward an explanation would be to highlight simply the notion that words as experienced in consciousness actually impinge on/ alter one's sense of the lived space of outer reality, that they, if you get close enough to them, and recognize (Dogen) that they are always exactly not describing what they propose to describe, alter reality in the sense that they break down all the supposed hierarchies and leave you with a kind of universality or all-inclusivity of experience, which both Leslie and Dogen are advocating and pointing to, in their various ways. This also relates to Leslie's life-long obsession with the horrible fact of violence, and her interest in animals — both of which appear in the Kiki Smith drawings. The kind of relationship to language/space/outer reality Leslie speaks of here would be the way you could cope with, and maybe overturn, the violence. Some of Kiki Smith's drawings for the book are reprinted in Leslie's essay collection *How Phenomenon Appear to Unfold*, which is where this quotation comes from. The drawings are oddly peaceful and tender. Which comes from Bataille's work on religion — that the consciousness of animals is Edenic, even though they are constantly eating one another. The title of Leslie's essay from which the quotation comes is "The Difference Between Fact and Experience," in which, as I take it, "fact" is the brutal hierarchical world, and "experience" is this intimate relationship to language (and time, which is in the human mind a function of language, metaphor). The essay ends with "…. approximates a state impossible anywhere except by being in one (can't be approximated except experienced by a person.)" It seems that for Leslie the social dimension of all this comes not from manipulating institutions or power (power is always terrible for Leslie) but through the utter transformation of the outer world from the inside. Dogen would completely agree.

PN: I'm intrigued by the invitation in the final passage of Dogen's "The Time Being" on page 58: "So enjoy the conceptual knots endemic to having a human mind, but do not pull them tighter." I've looked at two other translations of "The Time Being," and nothing like this appears; the whole last paragraph seems to be a wonderful instance of Norman Fischer stepping on stage. I'd like you to comment on why you chose this passage to take a great deal of liberty with and how the gist of that passage relates to the final quotation you chose from Leslie's work.

NF: Yes, you are right that the final paragraph of my "translation" contains broader liberties than I took elsewhere. I'm not sure why. Throughout, my intention was to add whatever I could, without going too far, to make Dogen's meaning (at least as I see it) clear for the contemporary reader. Dogen isn't writing a philosophical text per se, he's writing a practice text, a text that should be useful for someone actually practicing the tradition out of which he speaks. I've practiced Zen with Western people all my life and have a pretty good sense of what encourages and motivates them. There's a tendency to take Dogen too deadly seriously. To our modern ear, the tone of his writing seems possibly more austere than it actually is. I think Dogen is a lot funnier than he sounds! Anyway, I guess at this point I wanted to make clear to Zen practitioners that Dogen's message is an invitation for them to enjoy their lives even as they strive to see them clearly. Buddha's first truth is, All conditioned existence is suffering. Quite true, but pretty austere! So I want Dogen here to say — and I truly believe he means — that we should enjoy our lives as they are. Our human problems are also our delight, our fun.

The passage I juxtaposed here, unlike many of the others of Leslie included, that are theoretical or philosophical, is a pure poetic image, which is at the same time an experiential moment of time-being, in this case the fracturing of time, the past bleeding, as if present, into the present (which happens a lot, if you pay attention to it). Rain, lightning, a black sea, people on bicycles — and Leslie in this moment is also in a moment of childhood. That image, which is so stark, for me captures perfectly the bracing and dramatic sense of how life is when you recognize that it is always for the time being.

PN: One last quick question. The final page of *Magnolias All At Once* consists of a "Coda" linked with a passage of Leslie's. I understand the "Coda" is your composition. It strikes me as a beautifully condensed summation of your encounter with the writings of Dogen and Leslie. Am I on the right track?

NF: Yes. And something else too. As I read the passage it seems elegiac. Maybe the most beautiful aspect of "The Time Being" is Dogen's insistence that nothing is ever gone, ever lost, everything is always right here. That includes people in one's life (like, for me, Leslie) who are somehow as real as, or, in some ways, more real, more present, in absence, which we call death, than they were in life. The coda seems like a call and response that reflects this truth — the opening words call, Leslie's words, that I find haunting, respond. I don't remember exactly what I had in mind when I wrote that, but this is how it seems to me now, as a reader.

PN: Thanks for your time, Norman.

NF: You're most welcome.

Norman Fischer is a poet and essayist from the San Francisco Bay Area. His latest poetry collections are *Escape this Crazy Life of Tears: Japan 2010* (Tinfish Press, 2014), *The Strugglers* (Singing Horse Press, 2013) and *Conflict* (Chax Press, 2012), and his latest prose work is *Training in Compassion: Zen Teachings on the Practice of Lojong* (Shambhala, 2013). Forthcoming from University of Alabama Press is *Experience: On Thinking, Writing, Language and Religion.* Fischer is a senior Zen Buddhist priest, a former abbot of the San Francisco Zen Center, and founder of the Everyday Zen Foundation.

Leslie Scalapino (1944 – 2010) was an American poet, experimental prose writer, playwright, essayist, editor, teacher, and key member of the San Francisco Bay Area and national and international community of innovative writers and artists. She published more than thirty works of poetry, essays, novels, plays, and criticism. One of her early and most critically well-received works is *way* (North Point Press, 1988), a long poem which won the Poetry Center Award, the Lawrence Lipton Prize, and the American Book Award. Her most recent book is *The Dihedrons Gazelle - Dihedrals Zoom* (The Post-Apollo Press, 2010). A collection of her critical writing, *How Phenomena Appear to Unfold*, was published by Litmus Press in 2011. For more information, please visit www.lesliescalapino.com.

Dogen Kigen (1200-1254) was a Japanese Zen priest, teacher, and writer. Dogen founded the Soto school of Japanese Zen Buddhism, as well as Eiheiji monastery, one of the Headquarters Temples of the school. Dogen's writing has, for about a century, been considered in both Japan and the West to be unique in its stylistic accomplishment and intellectual depth, having been compared extensively to such Western philosophers as Heidegger and Wittgenstein.